Raise Up Your Praise!
(How To Be Better At Praising God)

Raise Up Your Praise!
(How To Be Better At Praising God)

Chip Vickio

First Edition

Cabin In The Corner Publishing

30845 Phillips Branch Rd, Millsboro, DE 19966

Contents

Preface

Do you experience days when you don't take even a moment to thank God or tell Him what He means to you? Don't feel alone. If you are like most Christians in our culture, you are so caught up in everyday issues and challenges that sometimes you simply forget to give God praise and acknowledge Him. When you do remember Him, it's most likely because you are requesting something.

Now there's nothing wrong with requesting something from God. However, praise is much different. When you praise God, it has nothing to do with you, but everything to do with God. You see, it's totally one sided – in God's favor.

I've never come across anyone who feels they are so good at praising God that they don't need to improve on it. Can you imagine? That would be crazy! No matter where we are in our ability to praise God, we should strive to be better at it. Why? It's simple - because God deserves it.

Do you know what I've concluded as one who has been involved in leading worship for more than twenty years? You need to practice praise to be better at it. You need to make a conscious effort to praise God daily, or you will be a mediocre praiser at best. After all, our praise to God isn't meant to be reserved for just Sunday mornings.

This book will give you ten suggestions on how to become better at praising God, concluding with 30 praise devotions to help you practice praise for 30 days. Then, at the very end of the book is "The Psalm 9 Challenge."

Be better at giving Him the praise He deserves, and start today in a conscious effort to raise your praise to a higher level!

Introduction

I bet you don't have any problem giving praise to a sports hero, especially if you are a fan of a particular sports star. No doubt you've seen fans at virtually every sporting event wearing the name of their favorite athlete on their clothes. It's a common practice in our society.

Regardless of the sport, we pour out special recognition to star players, often awarding trophies and medals. Their pictures are in magazines, newspapers, and television ads. Many become famous throughout the world. At live events, fans cheer a team or a person with enthusiasm and excitement.

The same thing holds true in the entertainment field. For example, a popular singer or musician will draw thousands of adoring fans at every concert. It never fails that when a famous entertainer simply walks out on stage before uttering a sound, there is enthusiastic applause. Standing ovations are not uncommon in live concerts.

Likewise, movie stars are adored by multitudes and honored with prestigious awards and accolades. They are cheered in public. They are idolized. They set fashion and cultural trends.

It doesn't matter whether it's an artist, a poet, a doctor, a lawyer, a politician, a philanthropist, or a scientist, in every profession you will find specific people who will be exalted for who they are and what they have accomplished. The act of praising specific individuals has certainly been a common practice throughout the ages, and will undoubtedly continue as long as man exists on this earth.

Now there's nothing wrong with praising a person if it is truly deserved. Have you ever wondered, however, why God doesn't get the enthusiastic praise that we give to mere man? I wish God would get the cheers and accolades that so many mortals get. Isn't it sad to think that perhaps man gets more praise than God?

The praise of God should be at a much higher level than the praise of man. God isn't just another highly esteemed person, although we should desire to make Him highly esteemed. The honor of God goes beyond the realm of this world, beyond time and space. He transcends beyond the physical and into the spiritual realm.

So why doesn't God seem to get the praise He deserves? I believe it's because of a general lack of faith in Him. The level of praise that we give God is an indicator of our relationship with Him. The more your relationship grows with God, the more your praise moves from shallow words to heartfelt expressions, and the more frequently you will praise Him.

Your degree of praise to God is directly related to your level of belief. When you give praise to God, you acknowledge that you believe He is who He says He is. You applaud Him, pay tribute to Him, and therefore, ultimately glorify Him. The more you come to believe, understand, and experience God's presence and influence in your life, the more you will be compelled to praise Him.

As a Christian, you should desire Christ to become famous. He should be the shining star and be given the spotlight in your life.

Who could be more important? Who could even come close? Can the praises given to man be compared to the praises that God deserves? Never! God is to be exalted above all and given praise that raises Him to the highest place in Heaven and on earth.

Why Praise God?

Why praise God? Simple - we praise Him because He is worthy to be praised. The word worthy implies great value and worth, which merits praise, honor, and glory. There are two main reasons why God is worthy of all praise: His identity and His ability. In other words, we praise Him for who He is and for what He can do. The more we understand His identity and His ability, the more compelled we are to praise Him.

The source of information regarding who God is and what He is able to do is obviously the Bible. Can you imagine what it would be like if we did not have the Bible to teach us about God? People would make up their own gods. The sun, the moon, and the stars would be worshiped. Nature would be deity. Idols would be bowed to. Sound familiar? Examples of idol worship can be found in the Bible as well as throughout the history of different civilizations. After all, there is a degree of majesty in the sight of Mt. Everest, and a sense of awe as we gaze out at the Grand Canyon. However, isn't it a travesty to worship the creation rather than the Creator? The Bible clearly distinguishes the two.

I remember my first experience of seeing the Grand Canyon. My wife and I vacationed in Arizona many years ago, and one of our goals was to see this wonder of nature. It's interesting that the landscape is relatively flat in that part of northern Arizona. From the approach we took, we couldn't even get a glimpse of it, even from the visitor's parking lot, until we walked up to the first lookout position.

Then the sight stopped us in our tracks. We, along with everyone else, were in awe.

As I looked around, dozens of people were sitting in silence, staring out at the vastness and beauty of it. Some on benches. Some on the ground, on a grassy bank overlooking the canyon. Who knows how long those people had been there?

The Grand Canyon is so big, you seem to feel its presence. It's hard to describe it. It's kind of a spatial feeling. I began taking pictures, but then realized it was impossible to capture the feeling I had of the canyon's surroundings in a photograph.

Isn't it a shame that so many miss the sense of awe and wonder concerning God? He may be invisible to us, but His presence is real and once we get to know Him, His vastness and beauty are overwhelming.

Without the Bible, we would be clueless as far as our understanding of spiritual truth. First, if you didn't have the scriptures, you wouldn't know who God is. Therefore, you wouldn't know whom to praise. Second, if you didn't have the Bible to show you God's authority and power, including all His attributes and works, then you wouldn't know why you should be praising Him. Do you see how important it is to be reading His word, the Bible? The Bible tells us the who and the why regarding praise.

I believe God created humans with an innate sense that there is a higher power, and people will tend to acknowledge it and worship it, whatever they understand that higher power to be. We were created as worshipers, and we will inevitably seek to worship something or someone. The incredible beauty and intricate design of creation itself is an obvious hint that there is a Creator God. Therefore, man is without excuse to believe there is a God, and without excuse to earnestly seek Him.

"For since the creation of the world God's invisible qualities—his eternal power and divine nature—have been clearly seen, being understood from what has been made, so that men are without excuse."

Romans 1:20

Although man is without excuse when it comes to believing that there is a Creator God, the only way to truly find Him is through the scriptures – the Bible. The scriptures, being the word of God, reveal to us who He is. The scriptures make known to us God's character and His nature. Because of this, we are able to correctly praise God for who He is and what He can do. The more we read the Bible, the better our understanding of God. The better our understanding of God, the stronger our relationship with Him develops, resulting in praise to Him.

Suggestion #1
Understand What Praise Is

Praise is Applauding

Praise is an expression of admiration. My favorite visual for praise is applause. When you praise someone, you applaud that person.

In our culture, applause is a very common expression of praise where there is a crowd of people gathered. It usually is spontaneous and in a sense, contagious. Applause doesn't require any words, although some shouting and whistling usually accompanies it, if the praise is meant to be enthusiastic.

As a worship leader, many times when our praise team finishes a song, the congregation claps. I sincerely hope that the reason they are applauding is more for the song's message, and not so much for our performance or for our talents. After all, to display our talents should be the last reason we are worship leading. Instead, we want simply to be effective in prompting people to worship the Lord. If we were to sing a song in which the lyrics described how great God is, and there is applause at the end, I always consider the applause to be like saying, "Amen!"

I'm hoping by clapping, a person is saying, "Yes, the words of the song are true, God is a great God!" I see the congregation's applause as a nonverbal expression that communicates, "We agree!" Even more so, I envision the applause at the end of a song as a corporate expression of praise pointed directly upward, as if we are applauding God Himself.

Besides applause being my favorite visual for praise, my favorite substitute word for praise is "Hallelujah!" It's a Hebrew expression which is translated "praise Ye the Lord" or "praise the Lord." I love it when someone spontaneously yells out, "Hallelujah!" Whether it's someone responding to a specific point in a sermon on a Sunday morning, or someone responding to seeing God's hand at work during the week, it's such a great expression that usually is spirited, enthusiastic, and vibrant.

Praise can be communicated in many ways – by words and by gestures. Regardless of the way it is communicated, when you praise people you speak highly of them. You give them the credit and the glory. The same is true with God. When you praise the Lord, you give Him the credit and the glory.

Praise is Boasting

Did you ever meet someone who is always boasting about God? I know a woman who seems to have something to praise God about every time I talk to her. She will praise God for what He did recently in her life, or praise Him for an answered prayer. She doesn't hesitate to give God the credit. Do you know what that does to me? It encourages me and confirms God is real and active. I love it when someone brags about God. Maybe her example is one we should follow. Let's be better at bragging about God!

Now boasting generally doesn't seem like a Christian thing to do. And it's not right if we are boasting about ourselves. It's a different story, however, if we are boasting about God and the hope we have in Him. We are supposed to be bragging about God! Once you are convinced of who God is and what He does, you can't help but boast about Him. Our boasting is a form of praise.

"In God we make our boast all day long, and we will praise your name forever. Selah."

Psalm 44:8

Boasting about God with other Christians edifies and builds up each other. It confirms our faith. It boosts our confidence in the Lord when we hear other believers talking about what God has done. Not only does boasting about God boost our faith and confidence in God among fellow believers, it can be a witness to other hearers who are not yet believers.

Praise is Spotlighting

For some strange reason, I have this fascination about spotlights. If I attend a large concert, the first thing I do when I walk into the theater or auditorium is check out the lighting, especially the spotlights. They are usually set far up in some corner balcony or ledge, with an operator assigned to each one. I'm always jealous of those people. I just think it would be fun to control the spotlight.

Praise is like shining the spotlight on someone. A spotlight will brightly illuminate a very specific area or person with powerful, white light. Sometimes during a concert or play, the stage will be darkened, and a bright spotlight will highlight one performer. The result is a tightly focused ray of light surrounding only that one subject. If the person moves, the spotlight will follow. Because of the spotlight, everyone's attention is drawn to that person, and there is a sharp contrast between the one who is in the spotlight and the darkened surroundings.

If you praise someone, you are personally shining the spotlight on that person. It's true regarding the praise of God also. If you praise God, you are personally shining the spotlight on Him. You are focusing on Him, highlighting Him, drawing attention to Him, and illuminating Him.

In the early days of stage production, before electricity, light was produced by heating lime in special containers placed near the stage. When the lime became hot, it produced a brilliant, white light that illuminated the stage. When someone was in front of this white light, they were said to be in the limelight. I tend to think of white light as pure light. When I think of the word glory, I think of bright, pure, white illumination. I imagine God in His glory is God in pure, white, brilliant light. Praise is a way to glorify God – to put Him in the limelight.

Praise is Exalting

To exalt someone is to lift them up, and to raise them to a level that is higher than anyone else. When we exalt God, we put Him on a pedestal. We place Him high above man. We acknowledge His superiority and His sovereignty. I believe that exalting God is not only raising Him to the highest level, it's also lowering our self in contrast. In other words, honest exalting requires honest humility.

When we exalt God, we acknowledge God's greatness, and at the same time, we acknowledge who we are compared to Him. When you look at it that way, you begin to realize that there is a large gap between the majesty of God and the character of man. Admitting that fact takes humility on our part. That's fine, because when we see the contrast between who God is and who we are, it's a confession of how great God is.

Sometimes if I'm leading a prayer, I like to use the phrase, "Lord, we lift You to the highest place!" By the highest place, I mean the highest level – the highest priority – the highest position. It's a statement of exaltation, honor and reverence. There's a passage in Philippians describing how God exalted Jesus for what He accomplished. Jesus humbled Himself to come to earth as a man and be obedient to death on a cross.

"Therefore God exalted Him to the highest place and gave Him the name that is above every name."

Philippians 2:9

17

To exalt God is to proclaim a praise that elevates Him. It ranks Him as number one, first place in everything.

Suggestion #2
Know Who God Is

Besides coming to know God from the way He acts and the words He speaks as found in scripture, one simple and concise way to get a comprehensive understanding of who God is comes from looking at the descriptive titles of God that are presented in the Bible. Taken collectively, these descriptions help give us an overall picture of His identity and His character.

As Christians, we believe that Jesus came to earth as God in the flesh. Therefore, in a general sense, by looking at both the descriptions of Jesus and the descriptions of God the Father, we get a really good, big picture view of the character of God. Thus, we obtain a well-rounded understanding of who God is. The more you read the incredible lists below, the more you will see how great our God is, and how He is deserving of all praise, honor, and worship.

Note: These lists are not necessarily all-inclusive. Some consider other descriptions of God as titles as well.

Old Testament - Descriptive Names for God

- Ancient of Days (Daniel 7:9)

- Creator (Ecclesiastes 12:1)

- Deliverer (Psalm 144:2)

- Dwelling Place (Psalm 90:1)

- Ever-present Help (Psalm 46:1)

- Father (Isaiah 64:8)

- Fortress (Psalm 144:2)

- Hiding Place (Psalm 32:7)

- Holy One (Habakkuk 1:12)

- King (Isaiah 6:5)

- King of Glory (Psalm 24:7)

- Light (Psalm 27:1)

- Maker (Isaiah 54:5)

- Salvation (Psalm 27:1)

- Potter (Isaiah 64:8)

- Redeemer (Psalm 19:14)

- Refuge (Psalm 46:1)

- Rock (Psalm 19:14)

- Shepherd (Genesis 49:24)

- Shield (Psalm 18:30)

- **Strength (Psalm 46:1)**

- **Stronghold (Psalm 18:2)**

- **Strong Tower (Psalm 61:3)**

- **Upright One (Isaiah 26:7)**

New Testament - Descriptive Names for God

- Abba (Romans 8:15)

- Almighty (Revelation 1:8)

- Alpha and the Omega (Revelation 1:8)

- Blessed and Only Ruler (1 Timothy 6:15)

- Consuming Fire (Hebrews 12:29)

- Creator (Romans 1:25)

- Father (Matthew 6:9)

- Father of Compassion (2 Corinthians 1:3)

- Father of the Heavenly Lights (James 1:17)

- Glorious Father (Ephesians 1:17)

- God Most High (Hebrews 7:1)

- God of all Comfort (2 Corinthians 1:3)

- God of Glory (Acts 7:2)

- God of Peace (Hebrews 13:20)

- King Eternal (1 Timothy 1:17)

- King of Kings (1 Timothy 6:15)

- King of the Ages (Revelation 15:3)

- Lord Almighty (2 Corinthians 6:18)

- Lord God Almighty (Revelation 15:3)

- Lord of Lords (1 Timothy 6:15)

- Majesty (Hebrews 1:3)
- Mighty One (Mark 14:62)

Old Testament - Descriptive Names for Jesus

- Everlasting Father (Isaiah 9:6)

- Mighty God (Isaiah 9:6)

- Prince of Peace (Isaiah 9:6)

- Wonderful Counselor (Isaiah 9:6)

New Testament - Descriptive Names for Jesus

- Alpha and Omega (Revelation 22:13)

- Amen (Revelation 3:14)

- Apostle (Hebrews 3:1)

- Author of Life (Acts 3:15)

- Author and Perfecter of our Faith (Hebrews 12:2)

- Beginning and End (Revelation 22:13)

- Bread of God (John 6:33)

- Bread of Life (John 6:35)

- Bright Morning Star (Revelation 22:16)

- Capstone (1 Peter 2:7)

- Chief Cornerstone (Ephesians 2:20)

- Chief Shepherd (1 Peter 5:4)

- Christ (1 John 2:22)

- Deliverer (Romans 11:26)

- Eternal Life (1 John 1:2)

- Faithful and True (Revelation 19:11)

- Faithful Witness (Revelation 1:5)

- Faithful and True Witness (Revelation 3:14

- First and Last (Revelation 22:13)

- Firstborn from the Dead (Revelation 1:5)

- Firstborn over all Creation (Colossians 1:15)

- Gate (John 10:9)

- God (John 1:1)

- Good Shepherd (John 10:11)

- Great High Priest (Hebrews 4:14)

- Great Shepherd (Hebrews 13:20)

- Holy and Righteous One (Acts 3:14)

- Hope of Glory (Colossians 1:27)

- Immanuel (Matthew 1:23)

- Judge of the Living and the Dead (Acts 10:42)

- King of Kings (Revelation 17:14)

- Lamb of God (John 1:29)

- Life (John 14:6)

- Light of the World (John 8:12)

- Living One (Revelation 1:18)

- Living Stone (1 Peter 2:4)

- Lord of All (Acts 10:36)

- Lord of Glory (1 Corinthians 2:8)

- Lord of Lords (Revelation 17:14)

- Master (Luke. 5:5)

- Messiah (John 1:41)

- Passover Lamb (1 Corinthians 5:7)

- Power of God (1 Corinthians 1:24)

- Precious Cornerstone (1 Peter 2:6)

- Resurrection (John 11:25)

- Righteous One (Acts 7:52)

- Ruler of God's Creation (Revelation 3:14)

- Ruler of the Kings of the Earth (Revelation 1:5)

- Savior (Ephesians 5:23)

- Son of God (John 1:49)

- Son of Man (Matthew 8:20)

- Son of the Most High (Luke 1:32)

- Spiritual Rock (1 Corinthians 10:4)

- True Bread from Heaven (John 6:32)

- True Light (John 1:9)

- True Vine (John 15:1)

- Truth (John 14:6)

- Way (John 14:6)

- Wisdom of God (1 Corinthians 1:24)

- Word (John 1:1)

- Word of God (Revelation 19:13)

As you can see from the lists of descriptive names, there's no one like God - not even close! Just looking through the descriptions is enough to prompt you to praise and worship Him. I'm in awe every time I look at these names. I love it when I show these names to people. And I love the response most believers seem to give when they review these lists. It's usually a "Wow!"

> *"Among the gods there is none like you, O Lord; no deeds can compare with yours."*
>
> *Psalm 86:8*

Suggestion #3
Reflect On What He's Done

You praise God for who He is, but you also praise Him for His works (past, present, and future). Breaking that down further, you praise Him for who He is, for what He has done, for what He is doing, and for what He will do.

If you start on page one of the Bible, you will begin to see what God has done, beginning with the creation of the world. If you were to list all the works of God, creation would probably be at the top. In the Old Testament and the New, you can read about dozens and dozens of events and circumstances caused by God. Miracles, intervention, and providence are demonstrated throughout the Bible. These are all examples of what God has done in the past, and they are reasons to give Him praise.

No doubt the most significant reason to praise God is for His offer of salvation through Jesus. The apostle Peter aptly puts it into words in the scripture below.

> *"Praise be to the God and Father of our Lord Jesus Christ! In his great mercy he has given us new birth into a living hope through the resurrection of Jesus Christ from the dead."*
>
> *1 Peter 1:3*

It's hard to top that one! And if you take it on a personal level, you should continually praise God for saving your soul! He has given you new birth into a living hope through the resurrection of Jesus Christ from the dead! Hallelujah!

We need to praise God not only for the big things like salvation, but for the little things also. Just recall what God has done in your own life. Look back at your past and remember how God has been good to you, how He has intervened for you, and how He has blessed you. Recount specific incidents where God has answered prayers, or worked things out for you, or provided for you, or protected you. Praise Him for it, and do it on a daily basis.

When you take a personal inventory of what He's done so far in your life, you will find He is truly worthy to be praised.

"Praise be to the God and Father of our Lord Jesus Christ, who has blessed us in the Heavenly realms with every spiritual blessing in Christ."

Ephesians 1:3

Suggestion #4
Realize What He Is Doing

Not only can you praise Him for what He has done in the past, you can praise Him for what He is doing in your life currently as well. God is not dead. He is not a God who only once existed in the past. He listens. He sees. He hears. After all, God is alive and well. God is real time. He is an interactive God. In other words, He actively is able to respond, in real time, to events in your life while they are happening. His hand can be easily and frequently seen working in your life, if you only allow yourself to be conscious of it.

Speaking for myself, I know that the more I begin to acknowledge God's influence and presence in my daily life, the more perceptive I am to seeing His hand at work in the future.

Here's a great habit to develop - when you do see God in action, praise Him right on the spot. For example, answered prayer is a great opportunity to praise God. When you realize one of your prayers has been answered, praise Him right away. Don't delay it. Stop whatever you are doing, and give Him praise.

Likewise, when you hear of Him working in someone else's life, praise Him right away. When you see the results of His providence or provision unfold before your very eyes, your praise response should be immediate.

There are several examples in the Bible of this type of praise response. In one instance, when Jesus was teaching in the synagogue, a woman was there who had been crippled for eighteen years. She was bent over and could not straighten up. When Jesus saw her, He called her to come close. Do you know what He did next? He healed her! Take a look at her praise response. It was without hesitation.

> "When Jesus saw her, he called her forward and said to her, 'Woman, you are set free from your infirmity.' Then he put his hands on her, and immediately she straightened up and praised God."
>
> Luke 13:12-13

I love the sequence of events. He laid His hands on her. She was healed. She praised God. Her response was simple, pure, real, and spontaneous. She praised God on the spot.

Another example of an immediate praise response occurred at the miracle Jesus performed at the city of Nain. This happens to be one of my favorite miracles. It's such a great illustration of sympathy on the Lord's part. If you notice in the story, no one asked for a miracle, and no faith was required. It was simply an outpouring and demonstration of compassion by Jesus. Here's how it goes.

As Jesus approached the city, He came across a funeral procession. A coffin containing a dead man was being carried out from the city gate. His mother and a large crowd from the city followed the casket. She was a widow, so she had no husband to provide for her. What made matters worse was that the man who had died was her only son, which meant she virtually had no means of support. Because she had lost a husband and her only son, she was now most likely destitute.

Something wonderful happens next though. Jesus saw the mother mourning. He felt compassion for her. He approached her and began to speak. He told her not to cry. Then He went up to the coffin and said, "Young man, I say to you, get up!" Immediately, in front of all the crowd, the dead man came alive, sat up from his casket, and began to talk! Can you imagine the scene? Look at the response of those who witnessed the miracle.

> "The dead man sat up and began to talk, and Jesus gave Him back to his mother. They were all filled with awe and praised God. 'A great prophet has appeared among us,' they said. 'God has come to help his people.' This news about Jesus spread throughout Judea and the surrounding country."
>
> Luke 7:15-17

That's right, their response was immediate praise, on the spot, without hesitation. I like the fact that their awe of what Jesus did prompted verbal praise.

Another time, when Jesus was teaching, some men came carrying a paralyzed man on a mat. They wanted to take Him into the house where Jesus was, but because of the crowd, they couldn't make their way to Him. Instead, they went up to the roof and lowered the paralyzed man down into the middle of the crowd, right in front of Jesus. When Jesus saw this demonstration of faith, He said, "Friend, your sins are forgiven." Then He healed the man of his paralysis. Look at the response.

> *"Immediately he stood up in front of them, took what he had been lying on and went home praising God. Everyone was amazed and gave praise to God. They were filled with awe and said, 'We have seen remarkable things today.'"*
>
> *Luke 5:25-26*

Not only did the man who was healed personally respond with praise, all the witnesses were amazed and gave praise to God as well.

Let's learn this lesson from the examples above: Praise Him on the spot when we see Him at work, and don't be afraid to verbalize it.

Always be poised for praise. Condition yourself to be quick to give God the credit He deserves by praising Him on the spot. When you realize He has answered a prayer, praise Him on the spot. When you witness Him intervening in life situations, praise Him on the spot. When you acknowledge the beauty of creation, praise Him on the spot. If you are in the habit of being perceptive of God's hand at work, you will become a great praiser and will not only glorify Him, but you will encourage others to see Him exalted.

There's no doubt about it, we should be constantly in an attitude of praise.

> *"From the rising of the sun to the place where it sets, the name of the LORD is to be praised."*
>
> *Psalm 113:3*

How often are we to praise God? Look at the following scripture.

> *"I will extol the LORD at all times; his praise will always be on my lips."*
>
> *Psalm 34:1*

That should be our motto. That should be our mindset – our habit. His praise should always be on our lips.

> *"My mouth is filled with your praise, declaring your splendor all day long."*
>
> *Psalm 71:8*

Looking back over the years, I remember many times praying for safe travels whenever I took my family on long road trips. Before I left the driveway, I'd make sure I would pray – for safety, for alertness, for God's angels to guide my way. One day I realized something. Whenever I safely reached my destination, I never acknowledged my answered prayer! I would pray before I left, but when I arrived at my destination, I always forgot to thank God. Now I'm in the habit of thanking Him and praising Him every time I arrive safely at my destination.

If any of my friends or family go on a trip, I'm praying for their safe arrival. When they get there, they usually text me to say they have made it safely. My typical text back simply says, "Praise."

Always remember to give God the credit. When nature's beauty, such as a colorful sunset, attracts your attention, respond with praise to the Creator. When someone mentions how God is working in his or her life, express praise to God. When you are alone express praise. When you are with others express praise.

A section of scripture from Psalm 71 gives a great example of someone who desires to give God praise for his entire life.

"My mouth will tell of your righteousness, of your salvation all day long, though I know not its measure. I will come and proclaim your mighty acts, O Sovereign LORD; I will proclaim your righteousness, yours alone. Since my youth, O God, you have taught me, and to this day I declare your marvelous deeds. Even when I am old and gray, do not forsake me, O God, till I

declare your power to the next generation, your might

to all who are to come."

Psalm 71:15-18

There is so much steadfast conviction in this Psalm. This type of attitude is a great one for all of us to emulate. I know when I read this passage, I want those words to be mine.

Suggestion #5
Remember What He Will Do

Get in the habit of praising God not only for what He has done in the past, or what He currently is doing in your life, but also for what He says He will do in the future. Remember His promises of future rewards and of things to come. They are all reasons to exalt Him.

Praise Him for what He will do regarding the biblical prophesies yet to be fulfilled. For example, praise Him for how Jesus will come back to gather His church, or how He will be victorious on the Last Day. Praise Him for how He will resurrect us, and how we will live in paradise forever with Him.

In addition to praising Him for the eternal promises of hope, praise Him for what He will do for us in this life as well. Think of the promises He offers us, like how He will provide for us and give us comfort, peace, and joy in this life.

> *"I praise God for what he has promised; Yes, I praise the Lord for what he has promised."*
>
> *Psalm 56:10 (NLT)*

Praising Him for what is to come in this life or the next is an expression of faith. The idea that we can praise the Lord for things not yet seen implies that we believe He will be true to His word. After all, faith is being sure of what we hope for.

"Now faith is being sure of what we hope for and certain of what we do not see."

Hebrews 11:1

Once we have this confidence that God will do what He says He will do, we will not only put our trust in Him, we will praise Him for His promises.

The positive expectation of the promises ahead can be called hope.

"But as for me, I will always have hope; I will praise you more and more."

Psalm 71:14

God's word endures forever, and his faithfulness to His word and His love for us will never fail. He will never leave us or forsake us. So praise Him for His love and faithfulness to come.

"For great is his love toward us, and the faithfulness of the LORD endures forever. Praise the LORD."

Psalm 117:2

Suggestion #6
Praise With A Sincere Heart

When looking at the examples of praise found in the scriptures, what you will find is that they are filled with sincerity, with humility, with honesty, with emotion, with the right attitude, with joy, with gratitude, with reverence, and with awe. That's exactly how you should praise Him. Most important though, is that your praise is from the heart.

Anyone can address our Lord with words, but unless it's meant from the heart, the words are worthless. God is always looking at the heart for sincerity. He is always looking for more than empty words. Simply going through the motions doesn't get it with God.

> *"The Lord says: 'These people come near to me with their mouth and honor me with their lips, but their hearts are far from me. Their worship of me is made up only of rules taught by men.'"*
>
> *Isaiah 29:13*

The above scripture is startling to me. It's scary to think that God looks at our hearts when we honor Him, and knows whether our worship is real or fake. My immediate reaction is self-evaluation. It makes me ask, "Is my worship, my praise, sincere and heartfelt, or am I just going through the motions?" It's good to self-evaluate, especially when we are compelled to do so by scripture.

It's obvious that God does not want our praise and worship to be strictly religious in the sense that it is just a matter of following rules and rituals. He wants our praise and worship to be real. The only way for it to be real is to mean what we say from the heart. His desire is to receive worship and praise from those who truly love Him and have a relationship with Him.

Praising God becomes more real when you realize you are not just praising Him for who He is, but you are praising Him for who He is to you.

A great exercise in seeing God with a relational perspective in mind is to go back and look at the lists of descriptive names. This time personalize them. For example, one of the titles of Jesus is "The Bread of Life." If you look at this title as it personally relates to you, then you would realize that He's not just "The Bread of Life" but He is "My Bread of My Life." Jesus is the "Good Shepherd" - this is true. More important, He is "My Good Shepherd."

The "Redeemer" becomes "My Redeemer." The "Bright Morning Star" becomes "My Bright Morning Star." "The Rock" becomes "My Rock." "The Light" becomes "My Light." "The Hope of Glory" becomes "My Hope of Glory" and so on.

When you insert the word "my" in front of them, you will find that the descriptive titles come to life.

To take the expression of praise one step further, try using a praise prayer something like this: "Lord, I praise You because You are my _____." For example, "Lord, I praise You because You are my Hope of Glory."

It's fine that the Bible teaches the who, the why, and the how regarding praise, but there is more to praise than just academics. What's really important is your motivation for praising Him. Ultimately, what the Bible really does is convict you and call you into a relationship with the Lord. Once you enter into this relationship, your praise is a natural byproduct of your closeness to Him.

Sincere praise is a natural result of believing in God, knowing Him, and seeing His love in action in your life.

The more you come to know Him and the closer you walk with Him, the more you will naturally want to praise, honor, and exalt Him. Praise and worship become your natural response.

Coming to know Him is more than just gaining information. It is coming to know Him in an intimate, relational way. Like any other relationship to develop, it requires spending time together – by talking to Him in prayer, and by listening to Him through His word. The deeper your relationship with God becomes, the more heartfelt your praise becomes – the more real it becomes – the more frequent it becomes. It's really all about love - His love for us, and our love for Him. As this loving relationship between you and God develops, it will certainly result in praise, worship, obedience, and service.

This is especially true when you realize how much He loves us. He has proven His love to be unconditional. After all, He sent His Son to us while we were still sinners – no conditions attached. Ultimately, our motivation for praise is love. We want to praise God because we acknowledge His love toward us, we acknowledge His desire to be in a loving relationship with us, and we acknowledge that we are in a loving relationship with Him in return.

Suggestion #7
Use Praise Prayers Often

Words of praise can either be spoken "about" God, or directed "to" God. When you say exalting words to someone "about" God, you are giving Him praise indirectly. When you say exalting words "to" God, you are giving Him praise directly. Both are praise, however in one case it's indirect, and in the other, it's direct.

For example, suppose you witness a beautiful sunset with someone and say to that person, "Isn't God such a magnificent Creator?" You are giving God the credit and the praise, but you are addressing the other person, not God.

On the other hand, suppose you say, "God, you are a magnificent Creator!" You are addressing God directly. It's more intimate, and has an aspect of worship associated with it. That's because your words are from your heart to His ears.

Praising Him indirectly has more of an evangelistic or edifying result. Praising Him directly is more relational. Both are good.

It's useful to be aware of the two different ways that praise is addressed - direct and indirect. Here's another example: look at the sentence from Revelation 4:8, "Holy, Holy, Holy is the Lord God Almighty." No doubt these are great and powerful words of praise. They are even used in

Heaven. However, if we were to categorize this sentence, it would be classified as an expression "about" God.

Conversely, look at Psalm 36:5, "Your love, O Lord, reaches to the Heavens, your faithfulness to the skies." This verse would be classified as an expression "to" God. Essentially, it is a type of prayer. When such words are sincere and from the heart, these intimate praise expressions directed to God are what I call praise prayers and are worshipful.

Once I was at a retreat for men that focused on prayer. It was a three-day gathering that focused on being better at prayer. There were sermons on prayer, private prayer time, and public prayer time. I began to notice that there were no sermons or discussions on praise in prayer! There were all kinds of teaching on how to be better at taking time to pray, or on the importance of prayer, but no mention of the importance of praise in prayer.

During the public prayer sessions, which typically lasted for one hour, anyone who desired would walk up to the front and pray whatever was on their heart. Usually men prayed for others or for themselves. There's nothing wrong with that. However, something refreshing happened when one man came up to the front and prayed exclusively a prayer of praise to God. There was no mention of himself or others in the prayer. There was no request for anything. His prayer was exclusively filled with admiration and praise addressed directly to God. He started with, "Lord I praise You because of who You are." Then, he just continued nonstop simply listing dozens of titles of God. Then he sat down. It was a powerful reminder that a prayer composed entirely of praise is refreshing, as well as uplifting.

Have you tried an exclusive praise prayer lately? It doesn't need to be long. Just take a moment to address the Lord telling Him who He is, or giving Him the credit for what He does. Practice it often. Give Him a prayer of praise. Use it as an expression of worship.

Besides giving God a praise prayer, it's also good practice to include praise statements as part of any type of prayer. We can find an example of this in the model prayer given to us by Jesus. If you look closely, you will find that it begins and ends with praise.

"In this manner, therefore, pray: Our Father in Heaven, hallowed be Your name. Your kingdom come. Your will be done on earth as it is in Heaven. Give us this day our daily bread. And forgive us our debts, as we forgive our debtors. And do not lead us into temptation, but deliver us from the evil one. For Yours is the kingdom and the power and the glory forever. Amen."

Matthew 6:9-13

Notice at the beginning He says, "Our Father in Heaven, hallowed be Your name." This is a praise statement. It declares that God's name is to be hallowed - to be holy. Then Jesus ends the model prayer with another praise statement, "For Yours is the kingdom and the power and the glory forever. Amen."

Perhaps we should get into that practice of beginning and ending our prayers, whatever the content may be, with praise. You'll find that it's a great way to pray. Practice starting your prayers out with a praise statement, and ending it with another praise statement.

Suggestion #8
Share Your Praise With Others

"Glorify the LORD with me; let us exalt his name together."

Psalm 34:3

Sharing your praise with someone else is so important. Why? It first indicates who you are as a believer. It can open up doors to talk about spiritual issues. Second, it can encourage others, and it can build up faith in those who hear it.

My wife and I once took a trip to Chattanooga, Tennessee for a vacation. There is a place called "Lookout Mountain" where you can drive up, park, and see magnificent views of the valley below. There is one overlook where you can see the downtown section of the city, the winding Tennessee River, and the distant mountain ranges. It's an amazing view.

As I walked up to the railing, an elderly man who was a complete stranger to me was standing there gazing out at the beautiful view. I stood next to him, and he said out loud, "How can anyone believe there is no God when they see this?"

To be honest, when I first looked out at such an incredible scene, I hadn't been thinking about God at all. However, when he mentioned God, it immediately changed my perspective. I wasn't just enjoying an awesome sight to see, I was praising an awesome Creator God.

That experience taught me a valuable lesson. Sharing your praise helps remind people that God is alive and well and that He deserves praise for who He is and what He does. When I hear someone praising God, it reminds me of my faith in Him. I just want to respond with, "Amen to that!"

Just think if we kept all the reasons to praise the Lord to ourselves, and never shared it with anyone. It would be terribly selfish. Praise not only edifies God, it edifies the church. It builds up – never tears down. Shared praise can also teach, enlighten, and inform, as well as encourage each other.

The apostle Paul was very good at praising God. Many of his writings reflect his praises. My favorite praise section by Paul is found in the book of Romans. In chapter eleven, Paul is writing to the Gentile Christians regarding their attitude toward Jewish Christians. He explains that both Gentiles and Jews receive God's mercy and salvation.

Then Paul goes off on what I call his "praise rant." It's fantastic! He goes off on a tangent that is basically out of context with the subject matter he has been addressing. It's as if he was writing his letter, started thinking about how awesome God is, then stopped his train of thought and began praising Him. Then, after he's done with his praise, Paul continues on with his teaching.

Here is Paul's praise statement:

"Oh, the depth of the riches of the wisdom and knowledge of God. How unsearchable his judgments,

and his paths beyond tracing out! Who has known the mind of the Lord? Or who has been his counselor? Who has ever given to God, that God should repay Him? For from Him and through Him and to Him are all things. To Him be the glory forever! Amen."

Romans 11:33-36

I love the way Paul just spontaneously shares his heart of praise right in the middle of his teaching. He seems to interrupt the flow of his letter to boast about God, but it shows his heart.

Have you done that lately – shared your praise with others? It's good practice.

Suggestion #9
Praise God In Bad Times Too

Why should we praise God in the bad times? If you look down through the lists of titles, you will begin to see why. Just to name a few: He is our Deliverer, our Ever Present Help, our Rock, our Refuge, and our Hiding Place.

In our life, when things happen, it's either because God makes them happen, or God allows them to happen. Some things happen by His providence and intervention, and some things happen by chance or coincidence. Sometimes bad things happen simply as a result of our bad choices and mistakes. On the other hand, perhaps some of our trials in life could be God's discipline.

Regardless of why things happen, either He chooses to intervene, or He chooses not to intervene. God is poised to work in your life immediately, or He is silently observing your life's events. What's important to understand is that in either case, He makes the choice, therefore, He is sovereign and in control. Sometimes just realizing that He is aware of what is happening in our life is comforting. One thing is for sure: our Lord is always with us as a loving Father, and is by our side in all circumstances. If we are one of His, we can have the hope that, regardless of our situation, He will ultimately use it for good.

"And we know that in all things God works for the good of those who love Him, who have been called according to his purpose."

Romans 8:28

Another comforting thought is that Jesus Himself understands exactly what bad times are all about. He experienced hardships, ridicules, beatings, pain, and sorrow. He felt all of our emotions, good and bad. It's amazing that God the Creator, as Jesus, experienced exactly what it was like to be one of His creations – man. In this way, He can totally relate to whatever we go through in this life. He dealt with conflicts, false accusations, threats, and slander. He even experienced physical death.

God the Father did not rescue Jesus from all trying circumstances, but ultimately used them for His glory. Perhaps that is true for us as well. Praise God that He understands us, and that He can sympathize with us in all circumstances.

We do not live in a perfect world. Satan and the influence of sin have corrupted everything, leaving consequences in the wake. The only perfect place is Heaven, where there will be no more tears and no more pain. Knowing the fact that God is faithful to His promise of a future paradise is something that helps us get through tough times. Our faith in the fact that we will ultimately have the eternal triumph allows us to praise God even in bad times.

"Why are you downcast, O my soul? Why so disturbed within me? Put your hope in God, for I will yet praise Him, my Savior and my God."

Psalm 43:5

"Praise be to the God and Father of our Lord Jesus Christ, the Father of compassion and the God of all comfort, who comforts us in all our troubles, so that we can comfort those in any trouble with the comfort we ourselves have received from God."

2 Corinthians 1:3-4

David certainly gives us the most examples of praising God in bad times. He has written dozens of Psalms that deal with his life issues. Perhaps the most well know Psalm by David is Psalm 23. The reason this Psalm is so well known is because it is commonly used at funerals. However, this Psalm was not written as a funeral dirge, but as a song of hope in dealing with life issues.

"Even though I walk through the valley of the shadow of death, I will fear no evil, for you are with me; your rod and your staff, they comfort me."

Psalm 23:4

Praise God for the fact that we do not go through bad times by ourselves, but that He is always with us.

Suggestion #10
Let Music Be A Praise Catalyst

There are many things that can remind us about God and the blessings He gives us. It might be as simple as looking at the beautiful blue skies and the billowing clouds, reminding us of our Creator God, and prompting us to praise Him. It may be someone talking about answered prayers, reminding us of all the times our prayers were answered, causing us to praise God.

Of the many things that prompt us to praise God, perhaps the most powerful and effective one is music. Music touches our hearts, our minds, and our souls. All through the Bible we find music and singing, and most of the time it is done in the context of praise and worship. When music and praise lyrics are combined, it is a powerful catalyst for worship. After all, music and melody were invented by God for His Glory.

When we listen to Christian music, we can certainly relate to the message of the song. Because of this, we can easily get into the mindset of praise and worship. So if you want to raise your praise to a higher level, increase your exposure to Christian music!

What's great about today's technology is that we are living in an incredible era of praise and worship music! Even as recent as fifteen years ago, things were much different. Unlike today, there were no iTunes downloads, no mp3 players, and no YouTube videos. Now we have vast access to all kinds of music, thanks to the Internet. There are more Christian musicians, singers, and songwriters available to us than ever before.

Tapping into this wide variety of Christian music can certainly help you stay in tune with God. Whether you listen to music on your radio, your CD player, your mp3 player, or even your phone, let music prompt you to praise and worship God frequently. Listen to Christian music as often as you can. It will set you up for praise. Let the songs continually remind you of God – of who He is and what He does.

Songs are not just catalysts for praise and worship, they are also expressions of praise and worship. In the Bible, there are several instances of songs being expressions of praise. For example, in Exodus chapter 15, you will find the "Song of Moses." He sang this song as an expression of praise when he got to the other side of the Red Sea, after it had parted and the nation of Israel crossed over on dry land.

In Luke Chapter 1, you will find "Mary's Song." It's an expression of praise by Mary shortly after she had received the news from the angel that she would be the one to give birth to Jesus.

Without a doubt, the one who was the most prolific song writer was David. Look at all the Psalms he wrote as expressions of praise.

Whenever you get the chance, express your praise through singing. I know, if you are like most people, you probably don't consider yourself to be much of a singer.

However, just remember that God is more interested in the condition of your heart than the quality of your voice.

One of the things that makes Sunday mornings so special is that it provides an opportunity where we can join in worship and praise, singing to the Lord. Take advantage of it! After all, singing with a group is much less intimidating than singing solo. It's also a great way to connect with each other and with God. So sing!

"Praise the LORD. How good it is to sing praises to our God, how pleasant and fitting to praise Him!"

Psalm 147:1

The Bottom Line

The bottom line is this: our God is deserving of all praise forevermore! There is to be no end to our praise of Him. It will go on for all eternity. That's right, when we reach Heaven, our praise will continue for ever and ever, so let's get a head start!

In the book of Revelation, the apostle John has a vision of the Heavenly realm, and do you know what he sees? Praise and worship.

> *"All the angels were standing around the throne and around the elders and the four living creatures. They fell down on their faces before the throne and worshiped God, saying: 'Amen! Praise and glory and wisdom and thanks and honor and power and strength be to our God for ever and ever. Amen!'"*
>
> *Revelation 7:11-12*

One more thing – if we remain faithful, there will be a time when God will praise us! Sounds amazing, doesn't it? Our desire to please our Lord will result in praise from Him. This thought should make us evaluate the way we live. Are we living to receive the praise of men rather than the praise of God? May it never be! Yet, if we are not careful, we tend to live that way.

"Yet at the same time many even among the leaders believed in Him. But because of the Pharisees they would not confess their faith for fear they would be put out of the synagogue; for they loved praise from men more than praise from God."

John 12:42-43

Yes, there is coming a time when those truly in Christ will receive praise from God Himself! It will occur on that final day when Jesus returns to gather His church – His faithful ones. On that day, as we rely on His grace and mercy, redeemed and covered by the blood of the Lamb, we will receive our recognition as sons and daughters of God, and we will receive praise from Him.

"Therefore judge nothing before the appointed time; wait till the Lord comes. He will bring to light what is hidden in darkness and will expose the motives of men's hearts. At that time each will receive his praise from God."

1 Corinthians 4:5

Until that time, it is right and fitting to praise God. He deserves all praise and honor and glory. Practice your praise, improve your praise, and raise your praise to a new level. Work at it. Strive to be a better praiser.

May your relationship with the Lord continue to grow closer until you meet Him face to face. When that final day comes, may you hear the same words of praise from Him as the words the master spoke to his servant in the parable of the talents (Matthew 25:23):

"Well done, good and faithful servant!"

And then, with all the saints, may you continue to sing unending praise to Him forevermore.

Appendix I
Practicing Praise For 30 Days

Throughout the Old and New Testaments, there are examples of men and women giving God the glory, honor, and praise. From Moses to the apostle John, from Genesis to Revelation, expressions of praise can be found. The Bible is a wonderful source of information when it comes to learning how to praise God. If it weren't for the Bible giving praise instances and praise statements as models and examples, we wouldn't be very good at expressing our praise to Him.

I am looking for a commitment from you - to practice praise for thirty days in a row, using thirty different praise models taken from scripture. This is an exercise designed to help you make praise a daily habit from now on, and to become better at acknowledging His presence in your everyday life.

It's simple. Just read one of the thirty models of praise each day for thirty days. These models are composed of a praise statement, a section of scripture, and a devotion. The praise statements are taken directly from the scripture for that day. What better way to learn how to praise Him than to imitate some of the greatest praisers such as those recorded in the scriptures.

You must initiate a daily regiment for your daily reading. Most likely, the best time is the first thing in the morning. However, pick a time that will work effectively for you. Also, the more you can glance at the praise statement, the better. Memorize it. Say it out loud.

Most of the scriptures in the devotions address God directly. For those that do, feel free to use them as your own personal prayers. Don't just mindlessly recite them in vain repetition. Each time you read them or say them, use the words as true expressions of your faith and belief in who God is. Believe what you are saying, and remember who you are talking to.

If you address God using each of the daily scriptures and do it with the right attitude and with a sincere heart, then essentially what you are doing is worshiping God in prayer every time. Although the goal is to make you better at praising God, you will find yourself better at praying as well.

Praise Devotion Day #1

"Hallelujah! For our Lord God Almighty reigns."

TEXT: Revelation 19:5-6 (Author – John the Apostle)

"Then a voice came from the throne, saying: 'Praise our God, all you His servants, you who fear Him, both small and great!' Then I heard what sounded like a great multitude, like the roar of rushing waters and like loud peals of thunder, shouting: 'Hallelujah! For our Lord God Almighty reigns. Let us rejoice and be glad and give Him glory!'"

DEVOTION

In John's prophetic vision of Heaven, tremendous praise is taking place there. He hears the word "Hallelujah" being used. It literally means "Praise God." Hallelujah is found only four times in the entire Bible (NIV), all in the nineteenth chapter of the book of Revelation. In this chapter, all of Heaven is in an uproar of praise as Jesus is about to return to earth to gather His bride, the church, and be victorious in His battle against Satan and all evil. This uproar of praise sounded like the roar of rushing waters, like loud peals of thunder. Every creature was shouting, "Hallelujah!" John experienced the ultimate pep rally! In this scene, there is so much energy, enthusiasm, vigor, and exuberance. When's the last time a spirited "Hallelujah!" came from your mouth?

Praise Devotion Day #2

"Praise be to the God and Father of our Lord Jesus Christ, the Father of compassion and the God of all comfort."

TEXT: 2 Corinthians 1:3-4 (Author – Paul the Apostle)

"Praise be to the God and Father of our Lord Jesus Christ, the Father of compassion and the God of all comfort, who comforts us in all our troubles, so that we can comfort those in any trouble with the comfort we ourselves have received from God."

DEVOTION

In chapter one of his second letter to the Corinthian church, the apostle Paul acknowledges that he has been through difficult hardships. His opening remarks, however, are filled with praise to God instead of pleas for sympathy. That's because he has personally experienced God's compassion and comfort in his own times of trouble. Because of that, he is motivated to comfort others. In other words, Paul is compelled to imitate God's character traits of compassion and comfort. You see, God is not merely one who is full of compassion. He is the father of compassion. That means He is the founder of compassion. He is the supreme example of compassion - the standard by which compassion is measured. Because of it, He is the God of all comfort. Let's praise Him for being such a God, and let's try to be like Him.

Praise Devotion Day #3

TODAY'S PRAISE STATEMENT

"You are worthy, our Lord and God, to receive glory and honor and power."

TEXT: Revelation 4:11 (Author – John the Apostle)

"You are worthy, our Lord and God, to receive glory and honor and power, for you created all things, and by your will they were created and have their being."

DEVOTION

There is a reason our Lord and God deserves to receive glory and honor and power. The answer is simple: because He is Creator. Spend the day contemplating why the rank and title of Creator is so worthy of praise. Consider what the word Creator means: author, designer, architect, mastermind, the one who brings something into existence. What separates God from all others is that He created everything out of nothing. He didn't create from preexisting matter. He created matter itself! If that isn't enough, He created everything by His will. What is really mind-boggling is that He didn't just create this physical reality, He created the spiritual realm too! Colossians 1:16 tells us that both things in Heaven and on earth, visible and invisible, were created by Him. Incredible! And get this, the "Him" in Colossians 1:16 refers to Jesus!

Praise Devotion Day #4

"Your faithful love is higher than the Heavens."

TEXT: Psalm 108:4 (Author – David)

*"For your faithful love is higher than the Heavens,
Your faithfulness reaches the clouds."*

DEVOTION

If God's continual and lasting love depended on our performance, we would all be in big trouble. If His love slowly diminished every time we messed up, stumbled, said or did the wrong thing, or didn't do the right thing, we would be gradually drifting away from Him as time goes on. But thanks be to God, His love is faithful. It doesn't diminish. It isn't conditional. He chooses to always be there for us. His love doesn't fade or fail, regardless of our performance. God's love is so wide and deep and long and high, it goes beyond what we can fathom. Praise Him for a love that is faithful and enduring.

Praise Devotion Day #5

"To your name be the glory because of your love and faithfulness."

TEXT: Psalm 115:1 (Author – David)

"Not to us, O Lord, not to us but to your name be the glory because of your love and faithfulness."

DEVOTION

Pride is a major problem for humans. We always tend to default to our prideful nature if we are not careful. We tend to boast about our accomplishments as if our successes were all due to our own hard work. This can be true even in the church. If a church is growing in numbers, who is really behind the success? Let's not take the glory. If someone is brought to Christ, who is it that really called that person to the faith? The bottom line is that God did – Jesus did – the Holy Spirit did. Let's not take the glory. If a Christian is maturing through discipleship, what is the true source of growth? Let's not take the glory. We need to give the glory where the glory is due. He must increase, and we must decrease. Not to us, but to Him be the glory.

Praise Devotion Day #6

"Yours, O Lord, is the Greatness and the Power and the Glory and the Majesty and the Splendor."

TEXT: 1 Chronicles 29:10-11a (Author – David)

"Praise be to you, O Lord, God of our father Israel, from Everlasting to Everlasting. Yours, O Lord, is the Greatness and the Power and the Glory and the Majesty and the Splendor for everything in Heaven and earth is yours."

DEVOTION

The term everlasting doesn't fit in our material world. Everything wears out. However, in the spiritual world, it is reality. Everlasting means endless, limitless, and timeless. When we exclaim to God "Praise be to you, O Lord, from Everlasting to Everlasting" it means that there's not enough praise to match what God deserves. He cannot be praised enough. The verse goes on to list five qualities: Greatness, Power, Glory, Majesty, and Splendor. Greatness can be considered significance, importance, and prominence. Power can be defined as dominance, authority, and capability. Glory can be described as prestige, honor, and fame. Majesty is nobility, magnificence, and dignity. Splendor is elegance, grandeur, and excellence. Not only does God possess all these qualities, He possesses them in abundant measure. Amazing.

Praise Devotion Day #7

"Your word is a lamp to my feet and a light for my path."

TEXT: Psalm 119:105 (Author – David)

"Your word is a lamp to my feet and a light for my path."

DEVOTION

As of this writing, according to the Wycliffe Bible Translators' website, about 350 million people do not have any scripture in their own language. These people have no access to the inspired word of God. Can you imagine that? This is sad because God's word contains the truths that allow us to come to know Him. Not only that, it gives us the ability to understand how to live life according to God's principles. The Bible illuminates our way through this world. In John 8:12, Jesus said, "I am the light of the world. Whoever follows me will never walk in darkness, but will have the light of life." How terrible it would be to live in a world where there is no scripture. Therefore, don't take the

Bible for granted. Use it to light your way, and remember to praise God for revealing His word to us.

Praise Devotion Day #8

"Our Father in Heaven, hallowed be your name."

TEXT: Matthew 6:9-13 (Author – Jesus)

"This, then, is how you should pray: 'Our Father in Heaven, hallowed be your name, your kingdom come, your will be done on earth as it is in Heaven. Give us today our daily bread. Forgive us our debts, as we also have forgiven our debtors. And lead us not into temptation, but deliver us from the evil one for yours is the kingdom and the power and the glory forever. Amen.'"

DEVOTION

When the disciples asked Jesus to teach them how to pray, He responded with the well-known model prayer. What many fail to notice is that He both begins and ends this prayer with praise. Take a look at the first sentence. Jesus starts off the model prayer by saying to the Father, "Hallowed be your name." Hallowed means holy, consecrated, sanctified and revered. Then at the end of the prayer, Jesus proclaims to the Father, "Yours is the kingdom and the power and the glory forever." What a great statement for us to imitate. Truly Jesus honors and acknowledges the Father in this wonderful model prayer. Perhaps we should begin and end our own prayers in the same way - with praise.

Praise Devotion Day #9

TODAY'S PRAISE STATEMENT

"Holy, Holy, Holy is the Lord God Almighty, who was, and is, and is to come."

TEXT: Revelation 4:8 (Author - John the Apostle)

"Holy, Holy, Holy is the Lord God Almighty, who was, and is, and is to come."

DEVOTION:

How about memorizing this verse today? Start out in the morning saying it. Repeat it throughout the day. It's an easy one. Memorize the scripture reference too - Revelation 4:8. By the evening, you will have it stored in your memory bank. When you have it locked in, you will have stored three basic truths. First, God is Holy, Holy, Holy. When the Bible repeats something three times in a row, you can be sure it is important. The words "Holy, Holy, Holy" give a powerful description of who God is. As humans, we sometimes stumble and fall short, but we can be certain of one thing - God does not fall short in His holiness. We can put our trust in that. Second, God is Almighty. That means He is all-powerful, and reigns over everything. He is all-powerful, all knowing, and literally, all mighty. Third, God is eternal. He was (existed) before all things, yet He is real and active in the present tense. Likewise, He holds the future, and will reign forever and ever. Holy, Holy, Holy is the Lord God Almighty, who was, and is, and is to come.

Praise Devotion Day #10

"To Him who sits on the throne and to the Lamb be praise and honor and glory and power, for ever and ever!"

TEXT: Revelation 5:13b (Author - John the Apostle)

"To Him who sits on the throne and to the Lamb be praise and honor and glory and power, for ever and ever!"

DEVOTION

When Jesus was about to die on the cross, He said, "It is finished." What He was proclaiming was the fact that His mission on earth was successfully accomplished. Jesus was faithful even to death on the cross. After He rose from the dead and then ascended into Heaven, He took His exalted place at the right hand of the Father. Now, all Heaven praises the Father and the Son (the Lamb that was slain) for what was done - God sending His only Son to die upon the cross for our sins. In this passage, we get a glimpse of what is going on in Heaven - continual, enthusiastic praise. Let's imitate their voices.

Praise Devotion Day #11

TODAY'S PRAISE STATEMENT

"You are God, my Savior, and my hope is in you all day long."

TEXT: Psalm 25:4-5 (Author - David)

"Show me your ways, O Lord, teach me your paths; guide me in your truth and teach me, for you are God my Savior and my hope is in you all day long."

DEVOTION

I'm sure that there is one particular trait that God loves in a person: a teachable spirit. The above verse contains four sequential requests: show me, teach me, guide me, teach me. Even though these are personal desires of David, they don't come about through selfish motivation. They are indicators of a heart that is open, a heart that desires a close and trusting relationship. It reminds me of the popular worship song, "Open The Eyes Of My Heart." Such a request suggests personal surrender and a willingness to know the Lord intimately. Are David's requests your requests? If not, they need to be.

89

We can't be know-it-all Christians. There is always a next step in our spiritual growth and development. We should always long to grow closer to the Lord no matter how spiritually mature we become.

Praise Devotion Day #12

"I will praise you forever for what you have done"

TEXT: Psalm 52:9 (Author - David)

"I will praise you forever for what you have done; in your name I will hope, for your name is good. I will praise you in the presence of your saints."

DEVOTION

If we could praise God for a thousand years, it still would not be enough. Remember all the descriptive names of God? How can we praise Him enough for who He is? How can we praise Him enough for what He has done? All we can do is praise Him and never stop. After all, isn't continual praise going on eternally in Heaven? Look at what God has done for you personally. He's loved you and rescued you by sacrificing His son for you. We can respond by giving our lives to Him, worshiping Him, and expressing our praise to Him. So give Him praise, and don't be afraid to share it. Praise Him in the presence of others. It's a great way to encourage other believers that share your hope and faith.

Praise Devotion Day #13

"For with you is the fountain of life; in your light we see light."

TEXT: Psalm 36:9 (Author - David)

"For with you is the fountain of life; in your light we see light."

DEVOTION

There is a legendary spring called the Fountain of Youth. Although it is mythical, people have set out on journeys to discover it. Supposedly, the fountain would restore the youth of all those who drank from it. There is a common story that the Spanish explorer Juan Ponce de León heard of the fountain from the people of Puerto Rico, and set out in an expedition to find it. Although he never was successful, the story goes that in his attempt to locate the fountain, he discovered Florida in 1513. We, as Christians, have discovered something greater than the fountain of youth. We have discovered the fountain of life: Jesus! He is life, and He gives us the light to see. Through

Him, we discover true treasure, and with Him, we receive true reward - eternal life.

Praise Devotion Day #14

TODAY'S PRAISE STATEMENT

"God, you are very great; you are clothed with splendor and majesty."

TEXT: Psalm 104:1 (Author - David)

"Praise the Lord, O my soul. O Lord my God, you are very great; you are clothed with splendor and majesty. He wraps Himself in light as with a garment; He stretches out the Heavens like a tent."

DEVOTION

Have you ever tried to envision what God looks like on His Heavenly throne? What kind of clothes does He wear? I know, it's silly, but we can't help but think of His throne room like we think of an earthly king's throne room. Do you see Him wearing a gold crown, or a beautiful robe of purple and gold with emblems embroidered throughout? Is He wearing rings and jewelry? Perhaps the best way to picture God is to see Him clothed, not in physical garments, but in spiritual attire: splendor and majesty bursting forth in all directions and with brilliant magnitude.

He is clothed with glory and holiness. He wraps Himself in light. What amazing descriptions of God are in this scripture!

Praise Devotion Day #15

"Because your love is better than life, my lips will glorify you."

TEXT: Psalm 63:3-4 (Author - David)

"Because your love is better than life, my lips will glorify you. I will praise you as long as I live, and in your name I will lift up my hands."

DEVOTION

The love of our God toward us is better than life itself. His love transcends the physical, and encompasses both the physical realm and the spiritual realm. His love is eternal, and goes beyond this life. In this way, His love is better than life. It outlives life. God's love is faithful and unending. Our relationship with Him goes beyond death. When we truly come to believe and comprehend this, our response is praise. We will be committed to praising Him the rest of our lives. We will be motivated to express our worship to Him.

Some express their praise and worship by lifting their hands upward to God. Obviously, it's fine to do that. After all, it's scriptural. However, if you're not comfortable in lifting your hands, at the very least, lift up your heart to God. He deserves unending praise.

Praise Devotion Day #16

"How magnificent are your works Lord. How profound your thoughts."

TEXT: Psalm 92:5 (Author - David)

"How magnificent are your works Lord. How profound your thoughts."

DEVOTION:

Over the ages, mankind has produced artists who have created brilliant masterpieces, and musicians who have composed beautiful songs, but nothing produced by man can even come close to God's marvelous handiwork. After all, who can create a beautiful flower or a spectacular sunset? Who can design and create a deep blue sea or a full moon rising? Who can command and alter the laws of nature? Man has its share of famous thinkers and philosophers, but no one can match the wisdom and understanding of God. All we can do is acknowledge Him, praise Him, and be in awe of Him. How magnificent are His works and how profound are His thoughts.

Praise Devotion Day #17

TODAY'S PRAISE STATEMENT

"Who is like you—majestic in holiness, awesome in glory, working wonders?"

TEXT: Exodus 15:11 (Author - Moses)

"Who among the gods is like you, O Lord? Who is like you—majestic in holiness, awesome in glory, working wonders?"

DEVOTION

The above verse is taken from the song that Moses sang after he experienced the miracle of crossing the sea on dry ground. The questions he asks in the above scripture are known as a rhetorical questions. They do not need to be answered because the answers are obvious. There is no god who compares to the one true God. No one even comes close. "Who is like you, O Lord?" Absolutely no one, ever. Moses just witnessed an incredible miracle along with the entire nation of Israel. With a heart of praise, he boasts about God, and describes some of His characteristics.

He knew there was only one answer to his question and one alone. Who is like God? No one. No comparison. No contest.

Praise Devotion Day #18

"I praise you because I am fearfully and wonderfully made."

TEXT: Psalm 139:14 (Author - David)

"I praise you because I am fearfully and wonderfully made; your works are wonderful, I know that full well."

DEVOTION

The human body is intricately and incredibly designed. Just think of the five senses and how they all work together. Consider how we can hear sounds, see the world around us, feel with our touch, taste flavors, and smell aromas. Even beyond these abilities, think of the mind and how we can reason, communicate, and learn. The more we discover how the human body functions, from its overall balance down to its microscopic complexities, the more obvious it becomes that we were designed and created. When we realize that God is the architect and the builder, we must do more than simply discount evolution. We are compelled to confess Him as Creator and praise Him for His genius in being our maker and life-giver.

What is even more incredible is the fact that we were created with a soul! Besides being mortal, physical beings, we are eternal, immortal, spiritual beings as well. Wow!

Praise Devotion Day #19

TODAY'S PRAISE STATEMENT

"He has given us new birth into a living hope."

TEXT: 1 Peter 1:3 (Author - Peter)

"Praise be to the God and Father of our Lord Jesus Christ! In His great mercy He has given us new birth into a living hope through the resurrection of Jesus Christ from the dead."

DEVOTION

After devoting his life to following Jesus, it was devastating for Peter to see Jesus being arrested and then crucified. He must have asked himself, "How could this be possible for the Messiah to be killed?" However, when Peter heard the news that Jesus resurrected, he and John literally ran to the tomb with anticipation and wonder. To know that the death of Jesus was not the end of the story was overwhelming, yet empowering to them. Peter's attitude quickly transformed from one of uncertainty to one filled with hope and vision. Everything started to make sense.

For the following decades, Peter would be totally devoted to his mission. Let's use Peter's words of praise to remind ourselves of what God has done for us. He has given us a living hope.

Praise Devotion Day #20

TODAY'S PRAISE STATEMENT

"You are my hiding place."

TEXT: Psalm 32:7 (Author - David)

"You are my hiding place; you will protect me from trouble and surround me with songs of deliverance."

DEVOTION

A hiding place sounds so secure, doesn't it? A child will hide under the bed if scared. It's sort of instinctive to hide when afraid. Even animals find a hiding place when they are scared or insecure. Do you ever wish you had a real hiding place? As adults, we seldom hide, although we may want to from time to time. We more often get away somewhere. The writer of this Psalm, David, had experience hiding in caves. Once, when he was hiding from Saul, he took refuge in a cave. Obviously, he came to realize that the only secure hiding place to be found is not a physical one, but a spiritual one - God. We need to come to the same conclusion. Nothing is secure in this world. However, as Christians, we have security that goes beyond this world. The Lord is able to protect us and deliver us from any situation. It is He Himself who is our hiding place.

Praise Devotion Day #21

"My lips will shout for joy when I sing praise to you because you have redeemed me."

TEXT: Psalm 71:23 (Author - David)

"My lips will shout for joy when I sing praise to you because you have redeemed me."

DEVOTION

What does it mean to be redeemed? It means bailed out - bought back - exchanged - paid for - purchased - let off the hook - released - freed - vindicated - absolved - made amends for - acquired - reclaimed - repossessed - recovered - compensated for. Can you grasp what God did? He made the first move! That's amazing. He redeemed us because He loved us, not because of anything we did. He redeemed us because of His grace, not because we deserved it. When we come to realize that God redeemed us and we are His, we have reason to shout for joy! Consider the debt of sin and the cost of the sacrifice required to pay for our forgiveness. The cost of our forgiveness? - Jesus' life.

Praise Devotion Day #22

TODAY'S PRAISE STATEMENT

"Exalted be God, the Rock, my Savior!"

TEXT: 2 Samuel 22:47 (Author - David)

"The Lord lives! Praise be to my Rock! Exalted be God, the Rock, my Savior!"

DEVOTION

This verse starts with the foundational proclamation, "The Lord lives!" What a rousing statement. It's filled with excitement. It's the basis of Christianity - that Jesus died for us, but was resurrected that we might live. Since Jesus died, rose from the dead, and ascended into Heaven, He is still alive today. He is still present even though invisible, and He is one day coming back. In the meantime, He is the spiritual rock that we can cling to. He said He would never leave us, and His words are true. He has defeated death. He lives! Praise be to my Rock. The Rock that is everlasting. The Rock that is solid and steadfast. The Rock that withstands all the storms. Exalted be God.

Praise Devotion Day #23

TODAY'S PRAISE STATEMENT

"Yours, O Lord, is the kingdom; You are exalted as head over all."

TEXT: 1 Chronicles 29:11b-12a (Author - David)

"Yours, O Lord, is the kingdom; You are exalted as head over all. Wealth and honor come from You; You are the ruler of all things."

DEVOTION

God is in control. Our Lord is King, and He rules over His kingdom, the church. It is good to proclaim Him as head over all. He deserves to be exalted. The word exalted means to acclaim, to raise up, and to elevate. He is in first place over everything. God rules! Not only that, He is the provider of all things. If those who have acquired wealth and honor think that it is a result of their own talents, hard work, and fortunate circumstances, they need to think twice. Who gave them the ability to be successful? Who's providence is able to intervene in their lives, lining up people and situations? It is God who rules, and it is God who provides. Wealth and honor come from Him.

Praise Devotion Day #24

"The Lord is my strength and my song."

TEXT: Exodus 15:2 (Author - Moses)

"The Lord is my strength and my song; He has become my salvation. He is my God, and I will praise Him, my father's God, and I will exalt Him."

DEVOTION

The above scripture is another piece of the "Song of Moses" found in Exodus chapter 15. He had just witnessed one of the most incredible miracles recorded in the Bible. Just when it appeared the entire nation of Israel was to be wiped out as they fled from the Egyptians, the Red Sea opened up to let them cross on dry land. As they got to the other side, God closed the sea back up, drowning the pursuing Egyptian army. Moses and the nation of Israel were saved. Can you guess what Moses did when he got to the other side? He praised God. With conviction and sincerity, he proclaimed who God was, and he made it personal. Moses proclaimed, "The Lord is my strength and my song."

How about you? Is the Lord the strength that gets you through this world? Is He the song in your heart - the melody that's inside you - the rhythm that you walk to? Then proclaim it, and give Him praise.

Praise Devotion Day #25

TODAY'S PRAISE STATEMENT

"I will meditate on your wonderful works."

TEXT: Psalm 145:4-5 (Author - David)

"One generation will commend your works to another; they will tell of your mighty acts. They will speak of the glorious splendor of your majesty, and I will meditate on your wonderful works."

DEVOTION

We praise God for who He is and for what He is able to do. We need to pass that down to our children and grandchildren. If we worship God ourselves, then most likely those that follow us will do the same. If we are worshipers, then there is a high probability that our children, and even grandchildren, will be worshipers. This fact places quite a responsibility on us. It means that we can influence generations down. Even though we may not ever meet or know our great, great grandchildren, our faith today can have an impact on them in the future. There are serious and lasting consequences resulting from how we live our lives. We can leave behind something powerful and meaningful - our faith and our love for Christ. Praise Him, and pass it on.

Praise Devotion Day #26

TODAY'S PRAISE STATEMENT

"I know that you can do everything and that your plans are unstoppable."

TEXT: Job 42:2 (Author - Job)

"I know that you can do everything and that your plans are unstoppable."

DEVOTION

Admit it. Believe it. Proclaim it. Job did. Short, but sweet. God is able to do anything and everything. There is absolutely nothing that is impossible for God to accomplish. The solutions to difficult life situations, which seem impossible to resolve in our own eyes, can be easily handled by God. Even the laws of nature can be temporarily overruled by the Creator Himself. Raising the dead, calming the storm, splitting the sea, and even stopping the sun's shadow are scriptural examples of God's intervention in natural law.

If He is able to do all these incredible miracles, temporarily altering the laws of physics and nature, surely He is able to intervene and work in our lives. If God has such power, nothing can stop His intentions and His will. It's comforting to know such a powerful God works in our favor.

Praise Devotion Day #27

"For you have been a stronghold for me, a refuge in my day of trouble."

TEXT: Psalm 60:16 (Author - David)

"But I will sing of your strength and will proclaim your faithful love in the morning. For you have been a stronghold for me, a refuge in my day of trouble."

DEVOTION

Throughout life, we will encounter times of difficulty. There is no escape from it. Jesus even said that we will have trouble in this life. However, it is comforting to know that when it does come, we have a stronghold and a refuge in the Almighty. Another word for a stronghold would be a fortress. Another word for a refuge would be a sanctuary. There is something interesting about the combination of strength and faithful love mentioned in the first sentence of this scripture verse.

These two attributes form a combination that gives us a sense of protection and security that are both invincible and unfailing. Knowing and experiencing His strength and faithful love results in our desire to sing of it and proclaim it.

Praise Devotion Day #28

"I still proclaim your wonderful works."

TEXT: Psalm 71:17 (Author - Unknown, possibly David)

"God, you have taught me from my youth and I still proclaim your wonderful works."

DEVOTION

Although we don't look forward to loosing our youth, there's a real benefit in growing older. The longer we are Christians, the more we can reflect on what God has done in our lives, and therefore, the more we appreciate Him. Sometimes we can't see God's providence in our lives when we are going through a particular situation, but when we look back on it, we see more clearly how God's hand was in it. If we are faithful Christ followers as we journey through our lives with Him, the blessings that we experience keep adding up. The more we acknowledge His hand in our lives, the more we begin to notice His workings. No matter how long we are Christians, His grace is still amazing. His wonders never grow old.

Praise Devotion Day #29

"How priceless is your unfailing love!"

TEXT: Psalm 36:7 (Author - David)

"How priceless is your unfailing love! Both high and low among men find refuge in the shadow of your wings."

DEVOTION

What in this world is really priceless? What is of such high value that it cannot be bought by the wealthiest person on earth? It is unfailing love. The Beatles once sang a popular song called "Can't Buy Me Love." There was a phrase in the song that said, "Money can't buy me love." It's so true, especially considering that real love is undying, unfading, ceaseless, and tireless. Unfailing love is truly priceless, and even though it can't be bought, it is continually sought after by both the high and low among men. It is highly valued by every human. Once God's unfailing love is found, it becomes a safe haven. We find refuge, security, and comfort in it.

Praise Devotion Day #30

TODAY'S PRAISE STATEMENT

"Oh, the depth of the riches of the wisdom and knowledge of God!"

TEXT: Romans 11:33 (Author - Paul)

"Oh, the depth of the riches of the wisdom and knowledge of God! How unsearchable His judgments, and His paths beyond tracing out!"

DEVOTION:

When you think of the depths of the riches of this earth, what comes to mind? I think of the valuable resources found on our planet. I visualize diamond mines that contain precious stones, or gold mines that hold incredible riches. I'm reminded of the vast oil fields that flow underground throughout the planet providing us with such an important resource. All these riches represent the treasures of the earth itself. However, these earthly treasures are ultimately limited.

After all, the riches of the earth are not infinite. They are confined to our globe. Nothing, however, can contain the depth of the riches of the wisdom and knowledge of God. He is immeasurable and limitless. Such vast qualities are truly something to marvel at.

Appendix II
Take "The Psalm 9 Challenge"

There are four Praise Commitments found in Psalm 9:1-2.

"I will praise you, O Lord, with all my heart; I will tell of all your wonders. I will be glad and rejoice in you; I will sing praise to your name, O Most High."

Psalm 9:1-2

Here's the challenge: memorize this scripture and commit to each of the four action items.

Commitment #1
"I will praise the Lord with all my heart."

The above statement is a great promise to keep. Praise Him with your all, with everything you are. Mean what you say, and make sure your praise is real and authentic, and not done out of habit, using vain repetition. Of course, the only way to really praise Him with all of your heart is to be in a loving relationship with Him. The more that relationship grows, the more you will want to praise Him.

Commitment #2
"I will tell of all Your wonders."

When you come to love your Lord, you will not only want to praise Him, you will want to boast about Him ("In God we make our boast all day long, and we will praise your name forever. Selah" - Psalm 44:8). Not only that, you will want to boast about Him everyday. You won't be able to keep quiet about Him, and that's not a bad thing. Remember, when you share your praise of God with others, it uplifts not only God, but it uplifts the person you share it with.

Commitment #3
"I will be glad and rejoice in You."

Commit to being glad. That's a simple but powerful statement. Sounds like a choice, doesn't it? Try saying out loud, "I will be glad." When you grasp what God has done for you, you cannot help but be filled with gratitude and thanksgiving. So be glad!

Not only should we commit to being glad, we should commit to rejoicing in Him. Remember, no matter what, even when your heart is breaking, your joy is still found in the Lord. Nothing can take that joy away. It's an inner peace, it's an inner hope. Rejoicing in Him transcends our life circumstances.

> *"Though the fig tree does not bud and there are no grapes on the vines, though the olive crop fails and the fields produce no food, though there are no sheep in the pen and no cattle in the stalls, yet I will rejoice in the Lord, I will be joyful in God my Savior."*
>
> *Habakkuk 3:17-18*

God's love is unfailing and unchanging in every situation. Praise Him for the joy and the inner peace that is found only in Christ.

Commitment #4
"I will sing praise to your name, O Most High."

When you get the chance, whether alone or in corporate worship, sing praises to Him. There is something special about singing, whether you can sing or not! God doesn't really care if you sing in tune or not. He cares about your heart, and somehow music and singing can open the avenues to your heart. One thing that makes Sunday mornings so special is that it can be a time when voices blend as one in praise and worship to God. So go and participate, and when you sing, sing with gratitude in your heart.

Take "The Psalm 9 Challenge"

Want to increase your praise? Memorize Psalm 9:1-2, and take it to heart. If you really mean what you say and take this scripture as yours, you will become great at praising the Lord. Not only that, I'm convinced your prayer life will improve, and your relationship with God will grow closer and closer.

"I will praise you, O Lord, with all my heart; I will tell of all your wonders. I will be glad and rejoice in you; I will sing praise to your name, O Most High."

Psalm 9:1-2

About The Author

Chip Vickio grew up in Watkins Glen, NY and moved near Rehoboth Beach, Delaware in 1978 with his wife, Francie. They still reside there. Chip and Francie have three children. Their son, Chris, and his wife Emily, are currently missionaries with Pioneer Bible Translators in Tanzania, Africa. Their two daughters, Sarah Polite and Loree Vickio, are Bible College graduates.

Chip is the Worship Leader at the Lewes Church of Christ at The Crossing, near Lewes, Delaware. He has led worship at that church for over 20 years. He is an accomplished musician, songwriter, and Bible teacher. If you were to ask him, he would tell you that he is a Christ follower and a family man.

Made in the USA
Middletown, DE
20 November 2021

53011887R00086